Learn Lemurian Healing

A Journey Home To The Motherland

By
Tiffany Wardle

© Vintage Wisdom Ltd

This NEW updated and rewritten edition was created and published by Vintage Wisdom Ltd, 1st February 2020.

ISBN: 978-0-9575351-2-1

All rights reserved. No part of this publication may be reproduced or distributed in any form or by any means without prior permissions of the author and/or publisher

The material in this book is based on personal experience. Although the author and publisher have made every reasonable attempt to achieve complete accuracy of the content, they assume no responsibility for errors or omissions. Also, you should use this information as you see fit and at your own risk.

Any trademarks, product names or named features are assumed to be the property of their respective owners, and are used only for reference. There is no implied endorsement by Tiffany Wardle, Tiffany Wardle Ltd or Vintage Wisdom Ltd.

This book is not intended to replace your own common sense, legal, medical or other professional advice, and is meant to inform and entertain the reader.

All photos by Bertie Carter

All rights reserved worldwide.
Vintage Wisdom ltd

Contents

Introduction - 6
Meet your teacher - 11
Tips - 17
The history of Lemuria - 20
Mount Shasta - 26
The fall of Lemuria - 31
Lemurian crystals - 39
A channeled message - 46
Amara the Lemurian priestess - 50
A new spiritual age - 53
Surrounding yourself with positivity - 57

Practical Exercises

Opening the chakras - 61
Lemuria Healing Symbols - 77
Closing down exercise - 101
Unblocking emotions - 105
Final meditations with Amara - 112
Quiz - 119
Notes - 120
Continuing your journey - 122

Introduction

Lemurian Healing Course

Thank you for joining me on this incredible journey to Lemuria. I am honored to have you with me on this journey. Lemurians are such beautiful, pure, kind beings and I cannot wait for you to bask in their energy. So welcome! The first thing to remember during this course is to take your time. Each chapter may take you a month to complete as there is no hurry. This course aims to teach you about the age of Lemuria and the powerful healing techniques that came from this ancient time. You will be given a set of powerful symbols to help heal yourself and others. During your journey to the motherland of Lemuria, you will be given information and healing from Adama, the head priest of Lemuria. The Priest Adama also has many messages for you threaded throughout these teachings. I hope you enjoy this. You will also read about other powerful, spiritual guides that will help you with your own personal healing techniques.

This course is different to other Lemurian healing courses as I have poured my own Lemurian healing in to my words. I am currently writing while I climb Mount Shasta, California. It is said that many Lemurians fled to this very mountain during the floods of the Lemurian age. As I have been climbing Mount Shasta, which is known as the root chakra of the world, I have collected even more Lemurian energy to give you to. As I sit on the mountain and take stock of the Lemurian energy around me, I add this energy to these sentences. I have connected through my soul to give you unprecedented, channeled information from many Lemurians including an angel guide who has joined me while I write this course. This guide is a true angel of Lemuria called Angel Celeste. This loving, beautiful angel has also invoked her healing energy in to this course to hopefully awaken some deep seated memories within you from the Lemurian age.

Rather than just teach you the Lemurian healing symbols, I aim to help you truly sense the age of Lemuria. My goal is to open your third eye to help you see the beings of Lemuria. I hope you also heighten your senses to feel Lemuria during this course. I hope your hidden memories of Lemuria resurface. The more you heighten your senses, the easier the healing journey is.

This course will also help with the following:

- Helping you understand the age of Lemuria
- Invoking the power of Lemurian healing energy
- Enhancing your connection to guides from Lemuria
- Encouraging your personal healing journey
- Healing any emotional blockages you or your clients may have
- Teaching you how to become a certified Lemurian healing teacher yourself
- Fully opening up the seven main energy points on your body
- Ensuring you understand each chakra point and the benefits
- Increasing your connection to Lemurian crystals

- Showing you the benefits of balancing your energy centres correctly
- Receiving insights from angel Celeste and other Lemurian guides
- Learning how to connect with your personal angels and guides
- Increasing your intuition in all aspects of your life
- To help you enhance your inner happiness.

Get to know your teacher

I discovered this incredible healing energy many years ago and want to share it with you. I have been drawn to Lemurian energy since my very first meditation class some years ago. Over the past few years, I have been pulled to different points on our beautiful planet to feel the Lemurian energy on mother Earth. I have always been interested in natural healing and I am drawn to ways the body can help heal itself. Therefore I was very excited when I learnt about Lemurian healing techniques and how a set of symbols can help us physically and emotionally.

As well as being a natural healer, I am also psychic. I have been psychic my whole life. I voiced my first premonition as a toddler and started to use tarot cards in the early nineties as a teenager. I always knew there was something more to life and could sense guides, angels and spirits around me. This made my connection to Lemurian guides much stronger.

I started to read up about Reiki in 2007 and learnt about the energy flow we call 'chi'. I always felt that I didn't have a choice in becoming a healer as healing picked me. Learning to heal others naturally felt like my fate. I feel truly blessed to be able to pass on to you the healing energies that are bestowed to me.

Also in 2007, I travelled to Japan on my quest for healing knowledge and climbed the mountain where Reiki healing was discovered. I meditated at the top of mountain for three days which changed my healing ability forever. I have never been the same since I became a Reiki Master as my powers seemed to increase once I was attuned to the chi energy.

After ten years of developing my gift, going to The Chelsea College of Psychic Studies, training in Japan and working in California as a healer and psychic, I then set up my own healing clinic in Knightsbridge, Central London. I worked on Psychic TV sending distance healing and giving psychic readings to thousands of viewers. I now have private clinics all over London, Europe and in LA working with the Lemurian healing energy all over the world. I work with certain royals, film directors, actors, singers and many others using Lemurian healing to help them on their path.

I have also studied numerous other healing techniques: dolphin reiki healing, past life healing, soul healing, crystal healing, EFT tapping and psychometry healing to name a few. I soon realised that it was time to encourage others to embark on their amazing healing journeys.

If you have gravitated to this course, there is a possibility that you too have connections with the Lemurians themselves. When I became a Lemurian healing teacher my connection to the time of Lemuria and Atlantis became even stronger. I am sure it will for you too. My life has become calmer and more positive thanks to Lemurian healing, I would love nothing more for this to happen to you also. I would like to teach you about my gift and I will not hold back. I would love nothing more that for you to become a more powerful healer than myself.

I will be working very closely with my angels and my guides through this process. Angel Celeste is with me now, she is adding her energy to mine to make this course very powerful. As an added bonus, Celeste is also giving us information about the Universe as it is and how we can help.

A new spiritual dawn is here. The Mayan Calendar is a twenty six thousand year calendar which ended on the 21st December 2012, meaning a more spiritual age is here now. By 2032 we will enter the golden age. Spirituality will be even more heightened around the globe. What does this mean for you? This means, we need as many Lemurian healers, Lemurian teachers, psychics, reiki healers, light workers and chakra therapists as possible to help others evolve during this spiritual dawn. This includes you. Join me now on this journey to open your mind to the age of Lemuria and become a very powerful Lemurian healer. I hope you enjoy the healing energy invoked within this course from the ascended master Adama, priestess Amara, angel Celeste and also myself.

Tips

You may want to practice with Lemurian seed crystals during this course, please note you do not have to have any crystals to become a Lemurian healing teacher.

- I would stress that stimulants including caffeine and sugar can decrease your concentration for healing so it is suggested to watch your intake during this course.

- Each stage of this course should be practised for at least a week before moving on to the next section, although there is no time limit on this course.

- Some stages may take you longer than others to go through, be patient as it will be worth while.

- Please note that you may find you connect better with one or two healing symbols rather than all of them. This is totally normal, we are all different types of healers.

- These Lemurian symbols can be used to help heal yourself and others. It is suggested that you keep going over each stage to help the symbols really sink in to your soul, I know I had to.

- Leave your ego at the door please. It doesn't matter if you do not feel the healing energy at first, let it flow in your own time. We all have energy flowing through us but feeling it may take time. Don't worry.

- You must 'close down' after each stage. Notes are listed throughout the course on how to accomplish this. You may find your own way to open and close, I have made suggestions throughout this course.

History of Lemuria

The Lemurian age ran for thousands of years if not more. This precluded the age of Atlantis and came to an end approximately twelve thousand years ago. Lemuria is said to be a sunken continent. This continent spans an area near Australia, New Zealand, parts of Canada and America including California where I am right now as I write this course.

The Lemurians have been described as being between eight and twelve feet tall. The Lemurians were apparently graceful, loving and wise beings. I see them with long flowing lighter hair. They are often sighted in white robes. I have noticed many of them have steely blue eyes, however this is not always the case.

After years of peace on Lemuria, Atlantis and Lemuria started to war against each other. The Lemurians differed in the beliefs of the Atlanteans. Lemurians believed that the lesser evolved should progress at their own pace whereas in Atlantis the belief system was that the lower vibrational or younger Atlanteans should be shown their place in a hierarchy. During these debilitating wars, the neighboring continents became more aggressive with each other. It has been said that the high priesthood in Lemuria were told that their entire population would be wiped out and killed due to this fighting with Atlantis. The priesthood was warned that Lemuria and Atlantis would collapse and sink within fifteen thousand years due to the negativity that prevailed. As Lemurians could easily live for fifteen thousand years or more, they would see this devastation and would still be around during the collapse of their beloved motherland.

Just before Lemuria sank, some priests and priestesses made a pact to 'go down' with the land. It is said that the flooding took place over night. Some Lemurians drowned in their sleep. Others were comforted by the priests and priestesses who were previously warned about this natural disaster. The leaders apparently sent healing into the crowds during the floods. It is said that the forefathers surrounded the people of Lemuria with a 'blanket of calm' while trying to stop any deep emotional wounds continuing into future generations. The priesthood sang 'Auld Lang Syne' as Lemuria sank. You may think you are singing Auld Lang Syne to wish in the New Year however, it is suggested that deep in our subconscious we are singing this in memory of the motherland. It has been stated that emotional scarring from a disaster such as this may take many life times to dissipate, but singing this song helped the Lemurians try to remain peaceful as they drowned. Auld Lang Syne was perhaps the last song ever heard on the land of Lemuria. This song could well have greater meaning: this song may be helping us keep a memory alive of our fellow Lemurians. If we keep their memory alive, our dreams to once again see the motherland and meet Lemurians may not be too far off in the future.

It has been written that some Lemurian leaders decided to take twenty thousand Lemurians to Mount Shasta in California, saving them from the floods. The majority however, sank with the motherland. The surviving Lemurians used their minds, seed crystals and sound waves to create a city under the mountain where I am currently sat. The remaining Lemurians have apparently preserved their culture under Mount Shasta. Records are also kept here under the mountain with regard to Lemurian history. There are many sightings of the Lemurian people at Shasta. They are said to be living in health, wealth and pure equality. As I am currently in Shasta I have personally spoken to numerous people who claim to have sighted Lemurians. If you ever visit Shasta, be sure to read the local news and talk to those who live here about the sightings. I heard tales of Lemurians being in cloaks and being eight feet tall. One lady saw a Lemurian and mistook him for a human. So there have been many sightings here.

Lemurians are all said to have a sixth sense and also do not need to speak. They can understand each other on a deeper, telepathic level. They used sound waves not only to speak but to also to make things, like whole cities. Lemurians are fifth dimensional beings meaning they are able to teleport themselves and manifest all they want quite easily. The Lemurians supposedly mastered telepathy and clairvoyance eighteen thousand years ago. The priesthood used technology that makes our modern day computer system look infantile in comparison. It is said that they control most of their technology with their mind. They apparently had planes or 'air ships' that flew them to Atlantis and other places. Reports suggest they could make boats move on water using crystal power. I hope many of us find even more evidence of their brilliance in the years to come. We have so much to learn from this incredible race.

Mount Shasta, California

As I write this part of the course from a coffee shop in Mount Shasta, I can't help but notice how pure the energy is here. I can feel the healing in the air as I walk around the town. The whole place feels very sacred. This area is full of angels, guides, ascended masters and Lemurians. When I first arrived I heard a choir of deep voices, it felt like they were singing from the Mountain and it felt like a warm welcome from the Lemurians. I landed here at Shasta on November 18th, 2012 which is the High Priest Adama's birthday! I feel the singing I heard was a celebration for him.

Research suggests that Mount Shasta is enveloped by two pyramids: one purple pyramid pointing to the Milky Way and one to the core of the earth. It is said that these pyramids focus energy to and from the Earth and you can use the energy for your own well being, for others and the world. Many people feel the 'call' of the mountain here at Shasta. This feels to me like the call of the Lemurian people, our ancestors, trying to reawaken us to get to the next spiritual age seamlessly. Mount Shasta is reported to be the new Lemuria. It is written that soon Lemuria may well reveal herself to us again. I hope we all live to see this day.

I have just returned home to the UK after climbing Mount Shasta for the second time; where I was accompanied by an amazing mountaineer for the climb. I climbed to approximately eight thousand feet. The higher I got, the more spiritual I felt. There is definitely a sense of healing that I have taken from the mountain and invoked into this course. I was taken to certain areas of the mountain that were portals straight in to Lemuria itself. Here I felt the city under the mountain and many ascended masters joined me. I felt a warm welcome home to the motherland when entering these portals. I felt this warm message was not just for myself but for the masses. I was informed that the motherland wants us to live in the moment more to help 'still' the mind. Lemurians want us to ignore the chitter chatter of the mind and notice the beauty in the stillness. They ask we all try this now.

I was then taken to another portal of Lemuria. This portal is called Telos. My mountaineering guide took me into a meditation at Telos and I was quickly met by Lemurians who took me down to Telos within my mind's eye. I heard running water like I was near a river, I saw many animals, it felt like a fully functioning city. I could see Lemurian people looking after animals and going about their business. I could see Lemurians working in a loving, beautiful way. It felt very real. I believe I was then met by Adama, the higher priest of Lemuria. We then had a conversation about passing on the Lemurian healing energies out in to the world. I felt Adama telling me he would support this healing course as it would be beneficial for many. Lemurian healing is a powerful, natural healing technique. I came away from the meeting with Adama feeling this Lemurian healing course can help heal the mind and body It was quite an incredible experience. I pretty much skipped down the mountain afterwards! The altitude sickness, the snow, the cold, the snow shoes, the snow poles and the exhaustion all evaporated after my meeting with Adama. This was one of the most amazing experiences of my life. Thank you for letting me share this with you.

The Fall of Lemuria

A One To One With Adama The High Priest Of Lemuria

Since returning from Mount Shasta, I have had many encounters with Adama. So as I sat editing this Lemurian course in a Chelsea coffee shop in London, Adama came in and sat next to me. In my mind's eye, he looks like a blonde haired gentleman in his thirties. His curly hair is shoulder length. His eyes are turquoise, large, loving, all knowing and mesmerising. His energy is so peaceful that it feels wonderful sitting in his aura. He is showing me two images of himself: One in a white robe, which is what I believe he would wear now as a guide. He is also showing me himself as a warrior in a brown animal skin skirt and he is holding a weapon that looks like a shaped stick. He is now laughing at my humble description! I feel the animal skin would have been worn on the motherland, before he ascended to become a spiritual master.

It then became quite apparent that Adama wanted to show me the fall of Lemuria. This next account came from Adama's visions that he shared with me in my mind's eye.

Adama then starts to show me these images and sounds:

I hear loud noises, I see people running, trampling over each other. I hear hundreds of people all running from something. The Earth seems to tremble beneath them. They look terrified and are all running away from their homeland. As I hear screaming, Adama shows me a woman with long dark hair and a flowing white gown. The woman is running past me in my mind, she has lost hold of her young son. The woman knows she has to run with the crowds but she is in torment, she knows she too will be trampled if she stops so she moves to her right, away from the crowds, calling her son's name. She is in woodland. Her son is there playing! She sees him, cries, embraces him and picks him up whilst playing with his hair, momentarily forgetting about the hoards of people running away.

Adama gives me the feeling that they are running from a natural disaster, running from mother Earth rather than running from a war. The woman and the child stay together holding each other. In my mind's eye they look like they are far away from the crowds. She no longer feels fear even though she may well die but at *least she has her son. She came to realise that without her son she would have no life anyway. So she stays, sat on the Lemurian motherland in the forest, feeling peaceful and calm.*

Adama feels as peaceful and calm as the woman described above. I feel so privileged that Adama, the high priest of Lemuria, has come to me today to show me the end of the Lemurian civilisation as he knew it. However he gives me the feeling that this story will have a positive end. Adama talks with love as he mentions Mount Shasta to me. It is written that some of the elders from Lemuria have moved on to other more secret parts of the world as the mountain becomes more popular. However, Adama is telling me now how important and sacred this place is. Adama now takes me back to the people of Lemuria:

The people are running for the boats on the shores as they feel the tremors getting more intense under their feet. I'm shown some Lemurians descended back to the Pleiades, their original homeland. I now see that some decide to stay and die naturally so that certain humans could have a natural Lemurian heritage. I'm shown others fleeing, trying to escape on boats. I can see warrior boats now, like Viking boats. They appear to have carvings on the front of each wooden vessel. I can now hear water, however it is not coming from the sea. I can feel Earth tremors, it feels like the start of a natural disaster again. I can hear people panic at the back of the crowds as they hear the water coming closer. I can now hear a large explosion and the Earth floor seems to move. I am now being shown a huge tidal wave. It feels like the end for Lemuria. Although Adama always feels peaceful and full of love, he has his head in his hands as he is showing this to me. In my mind's eye I now appear to be witnessing the sinking of the huge continent that was Lemuria. The Lemurians that were trying to get into the vessels have been washed away. The lady with her child in the forest would have perished by now. Adama tells me that others chose to 'go home' and naturally descended back to the Pleiades before this event took place. I am now told that the Lemurians often felt homesick on Earth and wanted to return to their original 'home' to the Pleiades. It is said they were able to ascend naturally if they chose, as they were fifth dimensional beings. Adama is now showing me that he led some of the Lemurian people to Mount Shasta, California, way before this event took place. He is showing me that he's sad as he was unable to take more Lemurians. His elders had already informed him that he was not permitted to take everyone. He is trying to explain himself to me now, even though he understands he cannot and should not feel guilty about this, as it was meant to be.

Adama is making me feel that the Lemurian energy is still very much alive. He says to us now "Why not use this energy in our everyday lives?" He tells us to "utilise this powerful healing to help ourselves and help others." He asks we attune ourselves to the age of Lemuria and start to feel Adama and other guides. By feeling the energy of Lemuria, we will open up to a higher conscious way of living and purify ourselves.

This course can help heal any emotional pain that has been buried within for so very long. You may not even realise that you are harbouring sadness from the sinking of the motherland Lemuria. This course will enable you to bring healing to every part of your being. Allow yourself to really feel the healing and embrace it in the heart and through the breath. Let your higher self and your soul heal those imprints and memories of the sinking of the motherland forever. Ask your higher self to assist you with your healing now.

Lemurian Crystals

Please note that this section is for your information only. You do not need to have a Lemurian seed crystal to become a healer.

During my time at Mount Shasta I came across pure Lemurian seed crystals originally from a Brazilian mine. I have one near me as I write this course. You do not have to buy one for this course however you may be drawn to, this is up to you. Lemurian seed crystals do not form in clusters and therefore stand out from other quartz crystals that are found in clusters. They may have a slight pink glow to them. It is said that they possess energy creating oneness and unity. These crystals possess a very feminine energy from the motherland. Also possessing a very intense beam of light source. They are excellent to work with when healing. They can help enhance your connection to your guides, angels and ascended masters. Lemurian seed crystals are good to use when wanting to open up clairvoyance with your 'third eye' and when you want to feel unconditional love.

Record Keeping Crystals

Lemurian Seed Crystals are also known as record keeping crystals, meaning they hold wisdom. The people of Lemuria hid many Lemurian seed crystals for us to find and gain knowledge from. Records and memories of Lemuria and Atlantis can be unlocked when using these crystals to meditate with. The people of Lemuria used these crystals to connect with the masses, a bit like how we use social media in today's society. Lemurians used crystals to speak to their Gods and higher beings. These records are said to exist within the crystals and apparently we can unlock these secrets the more we hold and meditate with them.

Meditating With Crystals

When meditating with a Lemurian crystal, information could well be revealed to you about this civilisation, the healing techniques, the feeling of unity on the motherland and the love they have for all beings. To meditate with such a crystal, you can simply hold the crystal in your hand or run your index finger along the length of the crystal. Take deep breaths and close your eyes. Ask a question while holding the crystal. The question could be about yourself, emotional blockages, your guides or worldly issues. You may choose to ask to see Lemuria. Wait a few minutes to see how you 'feel' after asking the question. This may not come easily and may not work the first time you try, so keep at it.

Crystal Grids

Lemurian seed crystals also work well in grids. Try using three Lemurian crystals to make a triangle and then put an obsidian crystal in the middle. An obsidian crystal is a powerful crystal used for protection, you may want to use this too. Using crystals with a group of people is said to be even more effective. Breathe deeply and slowly as you use crystals, as the energy from the crystals will feel very strong. Crystal grids are powerful and very effective. If you have more than one crystal, you may find that you can link in to the higher energies more quickly. This can help you obtain higher levels of Lemurian healing and Lemurian information.

How to programme a Lemurian seed crystal:

We are firstly going to look at 'stating intentions' or 'programming' your crystals. By programming your crystals you are making the connection between you and your crystals even stronger. Crystals help the subconscious mind to work more effectively. A crystal is an important tool for unlocking the hidden recesses of your mind: for example you may carry a Lemurian crystal on your persons for help with healing. This crystal would work even better once it has been 'programmed to help heal.' Imagine crystals are like computers; they are able to receive, store, and release feelings and psychic information. Crystals absorb our energy if we have them near us.

Please note you do not have to go out and buy a crystal for this section of the course but please read through this section.

How to programme a crystal

First we need to cleanse and clear the crystal of any previous energies the crystal may have picked up. To cleanse: place in salt water for at least one hour or leave out in moonlight for as long as possible. Or leave in the sun for at least an hour. Or use your own method

- Hold the crystal in the left hand (or in the right hand if you're left handed)

- Imagine a white light from your hand going into the crystal until you feel that the crystal has been thoroughly cleared of old or stale energy

- Decide on a positive thought form that is suitable for the particular crystal e.g. for good health, for healing or to help you balance your emotions

- Hold the image of you receiving this good health etc

- Focus your energy on the crystal and hold the intention for five minutes approximately

- Bring your right hand to cup the crystal (or your left hand if you're right handed) until you feel you are done.

A Channeled Message

Please wait seven days before moving on to this section of the course to ensure everything you have already learnt has time to sink in to your soul.

What is channeling?

Channeling is a form of communication between humans and guides, angels, masters and spirits. I translate messages that I feel, hear and see from those wanting to communicate. I feel the ascended master and priest of Lemuria, Adama wants to communicate with me during this course as he wants to be a part of it. So as long as angels, ascended masters, spirits and guides have an interest in communicating, the link is made and the channeling can begin. For instance you may want to channel your angels, if they agree to communicate, then the flow of verbal and non-verbal information begins.

The importance of channeling

I feel Adama encouraged me to go to Mount Shasta, California to see the new city for the Lemurian people. Adama has chosen to let us feel the healing from the Lemurian people at Mount Shasta throughout this course. He has also chosen to reveal some hidden facts about Lemuria. Without the beauty of channeling, I would not be able to write this to you now.

A Message From Adama, Priest Of Lemuria

"I am Adama – A humble priest from Lemuria. I want to help you understand the power of your mind. We Lemurians feel that you have not fully awakened yet as spiritual beings. We Lemurians can assist you with this. We would like to show you how to get the things you need in life with your mind. We want you to forget your worries, your fears and have courage that you are guided toward your correct life path. I Adama have invoked some powerful healing energy into this course which should help your level of consciousness. Your concentration level is very important while learning the healing techniques of Lemuria. Try and 'still' your mind as much as you can throughout your day whilst you are completing this course. Try to be fully conscious in the now. It is the conviction of your

actions that will help you become a Lemurian healer. This is a powerful healing which allows you to have more strength and courage; so become the confident being that I know you are. Feel my courage now, to help you".

Tiff's Top Tips

This is a very in-depth course that is not for the faint hearted. If you feel emotional (like I often do when thinking of Lemuria) thank the Lemurians for giving us this healing, take a break and carry on.

If you are drawn to Lemurian courses, perhaps you remember this time in your subconscious? Maybe your guides are trying to steer you to a higher consciousness? Maybe you want to increase your healing ability? Whatever the reason, conscious or otherwise, state the intention to find your answers during this healing course.

Amara Priestess of Lemuria

As a Lemurian healing teacher and practitioner, I have a very strong connection to the people of Lemuria. I have a huge connection and a friendship with a priestess of Lemuria called Amara. I feel privileged to pass this knowledge on to you. I work closely with Amara on a daily basis in my healing work and teachings. Amara is with me now as she channels through me to write this course. Amara is happy to be with us while we are becoming attuned to the powerful healing energies of Lemuria. Amara is a powerful priestess of the sea. Amara will also be with you to help and support you through your work. Amara's energy is amazing! Amara is now in a spiritual dimension and does not have to be on this Earth plane as a human being to assist those who want to learn about the age of Lemuria. The aim of spiritual beings such as Amara, is to help you to achieve your highest spiritual potential. The beautiful priestess Amara is filling this course with love and healing energy. Amara is a loving, nurturing spirit. I still have private one to one healing clients and she is always there with me when I call her to help me assist those wanting some healing. You can be with her too. Amara is particularly connected to Lemurian healers and lightworkers who may find 'normal' life challenging. You may find you are highly sensitive to lower frequencies and the current economic state, so call upon Amara to help.

Exercise

Close your eyes and take three deep breaths. Call Amara's name three times. Try and feel her energy. What do you feel? See? Hear? Please keep trying this all week.

A New Spiritual Age

Please wait seven days before moving on to this section of the course.

We have many Lemurians and lightworkers incarnating to help us through this current spiritual transition. According to the Mayan Calendar, 21st December 2012 was the end of this age and a beginning of a new spiritual age. 2032 will be the start of the golden age, so we are living in a transitional time. The Mayan Calendar is a twenty six thousand year long calendar that has just ended, meaning a new spiritual dawn is on the horizon. So you can imagine the power of this new beginning we are currently living in. During this transition, we are supposedly moving into the Photon band and in to the Age of Aquarius, meaning we will increase our vibrations as humans.

It is said that people with an affiliation to Lemurian healing are here to guide others through the changes that the new age will bring. A lightworker is a person who feels they are here to aide others and the planet, these are people like you. Those of you here to help with the transition of the new spiritual age can feel the Lemurian healing energies immensely. It is reported that this new spiritual dawn will be exciting as the vibrational frequency of the Earth is being raised, enhancing our spiritualism. Lightworkers are those who feel there is a higher purpose to life and feel like they are here to help. If you felt drawn to this course you may be a lightworker turning to spiritual work to help others rise from the lower frequency.

The 'new spiritual age' will not happen overnight. This is a slow process, helping us toward universal oneness and destiny. Now we are heading to the golden age, lightworkers will continue to be born on this Earth plane in order to pave the way for others rising up from the lower frequencies.

Reawakening

Are you finding you are becoming intolerant to those with a lower frequency to you? Lower frequency beings are those who may still be living a non spiritual / materialistic / fearful / negative life style.

Do you want to give something back? Perhaps you can no longer work without feeling you are helping the planet?

Are you drawn to healing or alternative medicine? Perhaps you feel like you are a natural healer and cannot explain this?
Are you thinking about becoming a psychic? Maybe you had some premonitions as a child or you have an excellent intuition?
Do you happily spend time alone? Do you enjoy being at one with mother nature? Perhaps you feel energies around you that others cannot see?
Do you prefer the company of animals? Are you drawn to veganism or animal rights?
Do you dislike animosity? Perhaps you feel other people's energy? Maybe you struggle when there are too many different people around you?
Do others find you a little 'different'?

I am sure there are many reasons you are pursuing this course, so whatever your reason I welcome you.

Surrounding Yourself With Positivity

People in general tend to be drawn to lightworkers like you. You may find that you are vibrating at a higher energetic frequency, giving off good energy that attracts people to you. As you become a Lemurian healer you may find that you no longer spend time with the same people as you have raised your frequency. This was a difficult lesson for me but one I had to honour. Follow your intuition on whom to spend time with socially while you encourage your spiritual growth. You may also find yourself spending more time alone with nature. Quiet time and serenity is also important so that you can listen carefully to your inner wisdom. This will then enhance your connection with your soul and your spirit guides. You may be a lightworker holding memories from Lemuria deep within your soul. Maybe you are feeling home sick and cannot explain why? Maybe you are drawn to learning about the Pleiades? Perhaps you always feel like you are alone in your opinions or that no one understands you? This course can help with many of your feelings or concerns and will help you lift to a more positive place.

Exercise

Spend this week meditating on Lemuria. Call in Adama and Amara to help with this. See what happens. Can you see Telos at Mount Shasta? Can you feel Lemurian people around you? Have fun with this. There are no right or wrong answers here. This is to purely strengthen your connection with Lemuria. This may take you a few days, weeks or even months. We are all different and we must go at our own pace.

Practical Exercises

Opening the Chakras

Please ensure you wait seven days before starting this section of the course.

Before you learn the symbols of Lemuria, it is best to open up your chakras. These are the main energy points on your body. We need to open up these points to attune you to the Lemurian energy. By opening up your chakras, you will become more in touch with yourself, more aware of consciousness and more connected to higher frequency beings. These energy points on the body keep you aligned with your true soul purpose. From time to time we all need to realign ourselves so we feel 'on track'. This section shows us how.

So now I would like you to ensure you are in a place where you are not going to be disturbed.

Hold the intention that you are now going to open up the energy points on your body.

Take three deep breaths in, each deeper than the last.

Start to concentrate only on your breath and forget all your other worldly worries. Just focus on the here and now.

Before every Lemurian healing session, it is a good idea to state the intention that you are going to now open up your energy points.

I am going to show you a very powerful opening up sequence that includes sounds and mudras (hand positions). The mudras have the power to send more energy to particular chakras. To enhance the effect, sounds are chanted. These sounds are from Sanskrit letters. When you chant these words, you are helping to activate all of your main energy points in your body. You may have your own way of opening up, however please read this section anyway.

For pronunciation, keep in mind that:

the 'A' is pronounced "ah"

the 'M' is pronounced "mng" ("ng" like in 'king').

1. Open the Base Chakra

Let the tips of your thumb and index finger touch.

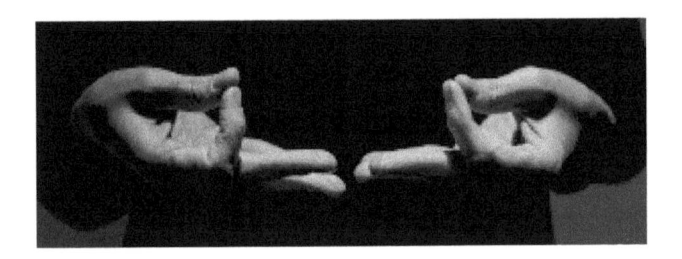

- Concentrate on the root / base chakra which is at the base of the spine.
- Focus all of your energy on this part of your body.
- Think of the colour red swirling in a circular motion.

- Hold the intention to open this up.
- Chant the sound LAM to help with practical skills.
- Once you have done this approximately five times (with five breaths) you can move on to the next chakra.

2. Open the Sacral Chakra

Put your hands in your lap, palms up, on top of each other. Left hand underneath, it's palm touching the back of the fingers of the right hand. The tips of the thumbs touch gently.

- Concentrate on the sacral chakra which is about an inch below the navel.
- Focus all your energy on this area.

- Think of the colour orange swirling in a circular motion.
- Chant the sound VAM to help with creativity.
- Hold the intention to open up your sacral chakra.
- Do this five times please before moving on.

3. Open the Solar Plexus Chakra

Put your hands just above your navel. Let the fingers join at the tops, all pointing away from you. Cross the thumbs. It is important to straighten the fingers.

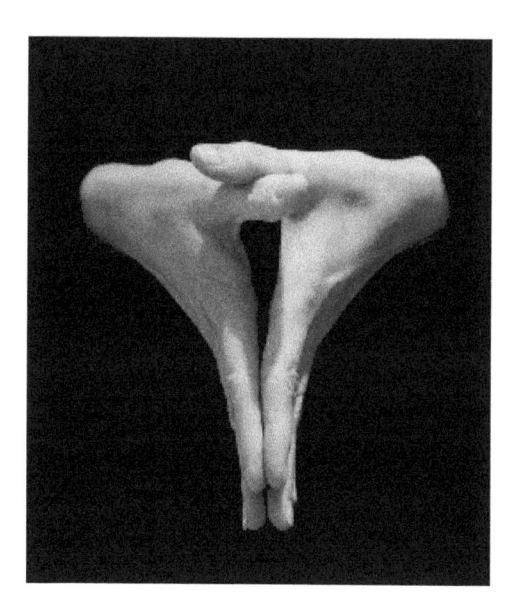

- Focus your energy here by concentrating on the area one inch above the navel called the solar plexus.
- Hold the intention to open up the solar plexus fully.
- Think of the colour yellow swirling in a circular motion.
- Chant the sound RAM to help with your intuition.
- Please repeat this five times.

4. Open the Heart Chakra

Sit cross-legged. Let the tips of your index finger and thumb touch. Put your left hand on your left knee and your right hand in front of the lower part of your breast bone (so a bit above the solar plexus).

- Concentrate on the heart chakra which is level with the heart at the centre of your chest.
- Hold the intention to open up your heart chakra.
- Concentrate on the colours green and pink together swirling in a circular motion.
- Chant the sound YAM to help open your heart.
- Try this at least five times until moving on.

5. Open the Throat Chakra

Cross your fingers on the inside of your hands, without the thumbs. Let the thumbs touch at the tops.

- Concentrate on the throat chakra which is at the middle point of your throat.

- Focus all of your energy on this part of your body.
- Think of the colour turquoise swirling in a circular motion.

- Hold the intention to open the throat chakra.

- Chant the sound HAM to help with communication.
- Try this five times.

6. Open the Third Eye Chakra

Put your hands over your third eye chakra (middle of your forehead). The fingers should be straight and should touch at the tops, pointing forward. The thumbs point towards you as much as they can and the thumbs should touch at the tops.

- Concentrate on the third eye chakra slightly above the point between the eyebrows.
- Think of the colour indigo swirling in a circular motion.
- Focus all of your energy at this point on your body.
- Hold the intention to open your third eye.
- Chant the sound AUM to help with your psychic sight.
- Try this five times.

7. Open the Crown Chakra

Put your hands just above your head, this is where the crown chakra is. Let the ring fingers point up, touching at their tops. Cross the rest of your fingers as much as you can (this isn't easy) with the left thumb underneath the right.

- Focus all of your energy at your crown chakra point just above your head.

- Concentrate on the colour violet swirling in a circular motion.

- Hold the intention to open your crown chakra.

- Chant the sound NG. This is pronounced like the word 'King' without the 'Ki'. Do this to help connect to spirit.

- Please do this five times. You are now fully opened up.

Tiffs Top Tips

You may have felt resistance during the opening up exercise. Or you may have had to try this a few times before feeling anything. This is OK! Try and feel where the resistance is in your body. Ask yourself why is there a resistance to opening the chakras? Hold the intention to release these blockages. Keep practising the opening exercise.

Exercise

Try the opening up sequence five times this week. Please wait seven days before you move on to the next section of this course.

Lemurian Healing Symbols

Now that you have learnt how to open up your chakras you are ready to start learning the Lemurian healing symbols. You are now going to learn a series of seven symbols to help heal yourself. If you choose to be attuned by myself, you will also be able to teach this powerful healing system. When attuned, the symbols will be imprinted on your energy field. The seven symbols represent different aspects of universal energy brought to us from Amara. After attunement, you may then trace these symbols over your client's chakra points as well.

AMARA

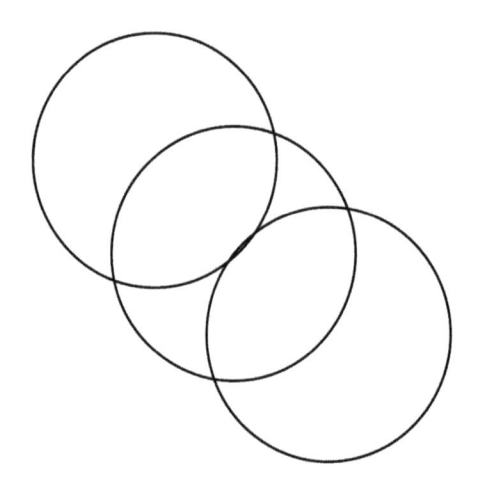

Symbol name: Amara

Meaning: Support, nurture, inspiration

Symbol chant: AM - AH - RAH

You can use this for all types of healing as this is the master symbol.

Process:
- Ensure you are sitting or lying comfortably
- Use the Amara symbol first before going on to use the other symbols below if you wish to
- Take three deep breaths, each deeper than the last
- Say AMARA slowly and with the intention to invoke her powerful energy to heal
- Trace this symbol on each of your palms
- See the symbol in your mind over and over again
- Keep saying the word Amara and continue this for five to ten minutes or as long as you feel necessary

- Try to 'feel' Amara close to you, this may take you a few attempts to perfect
- Ask Amara in your mind to be with you during the healing session while you trace this over your chakras
- The Amara symbol is the master Lemurian healing symbol. When you are attuned and not before, you can trace this symbol on both hands and then over your client's chakra energy points
- The energy of Amara then stays with you during the whole healing session
- Amara has a peaceful and loving energy, this energy will then go in to you or your client

OCEAN OF LOVE

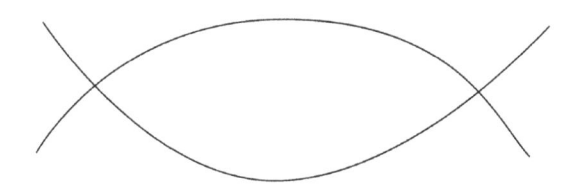

Symbol name: Ocean of Love

Meaning: Peace, rejuvenation

Symbol chant: MAH – NAHM – RAH

You can use this symbol for unconditional love. Use this in times of stress and discomfort to bring huge relief. This can help with anxiety or worry. This is also good for sleepless nights or anxiety. When using this symbol, an overwhelming feeling of love may come over you.

Process:
- Ensure you are sitting or lying comfortably
- Ask Amara in your mind to be with you during the healing session
- Take three deep breaths, each deeper than the last
- Say MAH – NAHM – RAH slowly and with intent
- Trace this symbol on each of your palms
- See the symbol in your mind over and over again
- Keep saying the word MAH – NAHM – RAH with the intention to invoke powerful Lemurian healing for peace
- Continue this for five to ten minutes or as long as you feel necessary and trace over your chakras
- Try to feel relaxed as you keep seeing the

symbol. Once you are attuned you can trace this symbol on a client's chakra points
• You or your client will eventually feel relaxed and calm, you may feel very loved too. This may take you a few sessions to perfect

INDIGO WAVE

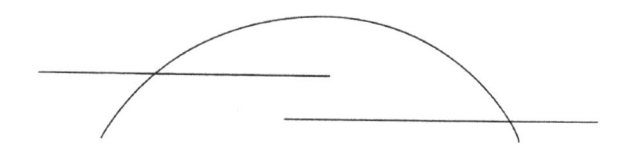

Symbol name: Indigo Wave

Meaning: Confidence.

Symbol Chant: LAH - NAHM - RA

Use this symbol for confidence. This is for increasing your self esteem. This can be used for clients who are starting a new venture, going for a job interview or changing large elements of their lives for example. Feel yourself filling up with confidence and then keep giving that confident energy to you or to your client.

Process:
• Ensure you are sitting or lying comfortably
• Ask Amara in your mind to be with you during the healing session
• I would suggest using this symbol for confidence when you need it most, so start feeling confident before using it.
 • Take three deep breaths, each deeper than the last

- Say LAH - NAHM - RA slowly and with intent.
- Trace this symbol on each of your palms and then over your chakras
- See the symbol in your mind over and over again
- Keep saying the word LAH - NAHM - RA with the intention to invoke powerful Lemurian healing and confidence for you or your client
- Continue this for five to ten minutes or as long as you feel necessary
- See how confident you feel for the rest of the day. When you have been attuned to this symbol, you can trace this on to your clients energy points.

SEA OF STARS

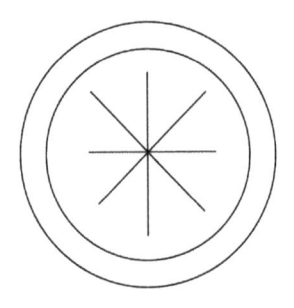

Symbol name: Sea of Stars

Meaning: Reconnecting to home

Symbol chant: OOO - NAHM - RAH

This is one of my favourite symbols. This will help bring you messages from the motherland of

Lemuria and from other galaxies. This symbol can help you realise why you are here and help with your true path in this life time. This can help you reconnect to your Lemurian roots. This may also help with your destiny. Maybe you feel homesick and you're not sure why? Perhaps you feel disconnected from the motherland Lemuria? The lower frequencies on this Earth can do this to you. You can use this symbol to feel the higher energy of the motherland and to feel the galaxy the Pleiades, the original home of the Lemurians.

Process:
- Ensure you are sitting or lying comfortably
- Ask Amara in your mind to be with you during the healing session
- Take three deep breaths, each deeper than the last

- Say OOO - NAHM- RAH slowly and with intent
- Trace this symbol on each of your palms and chakras
- See the symbol in your mind over and over again
- Keep saying the word OOO - NAHM - RAH with the intention to invoke powerful Lemurian healing
- Continue this for five to ten minutes or as long as you feel necessary
- See how connected to the world you feel for the rest of the day. When attuned, you can use this symbol on your client's chakra points to help them feel more connected to the motherland.

DOLPHIN

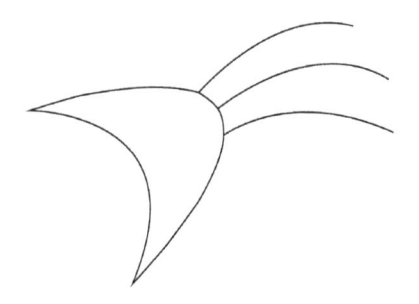

Symbol name: Dolphin

Meaning: Joy, hope, innocence

Symbol chant: SOO - MAH - RAH

The dolphin connection makes people happy and joyous. This symbol helps to rekindle a childlike free-spirit in you and your clients. When accredited, use this on clients who are feeling a little low. Growing up can have huge effects on us, this will help us re-live our childhood dreams, giving us the spirit of a dolphin which is free, happy and hopeful.

Process:
• Ensure you are sitting or lying comfortably
• Ask Amara in your mind to be with you during the healing session
• I would suggest using this symbol to feel more free-spirited and joyous
• Take three deep breaths, each deeper than the last

- Say SOO - MAH - RAH slowly and with intent
- Trace this symbol on each of your palms and chakras
- See the symbol in your mind over and over again
- Keep saying the word SOO - MAH - RAH with the intention to invoke powerful Lemurian healing for joy
- Continue this for five to ten minutes or as long as you feel necessary
- See how happy, playful and carefree you can be for the rest of the week. You can trace this on your clients chakras once you are attuned, to help them feel more free.

SHELL

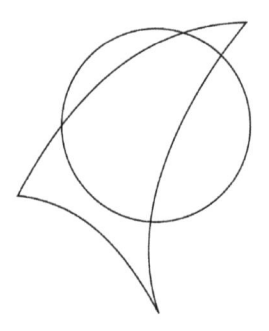

Symbol name: Shell

Meaning: Protection, security

Symbol chant: SHAH - TAHM – RAH

Use this for your own daily protection. You may

feel the heaviness from the current economic climate, maybe from your work place or from being around others with negative tendencies. Do you feel insecure from past hurts or previous relationships? This symbol can help with these issues. This will help you re-gain a higher energy level. This symbol helps to protect from stress when moving house, change of job or relationship for example. As you are a lightworker and healer, you may have a tendency to pick up on other people's energy. This will help you and your clients protect yourselves from lower vibrations.

Process:
• Ensure you are sitting or lying comfortably
• Ask Amara in your mind to be with you during the healing session
• I would suggest using this symbol for protection for you and your clients

- Take three deep breaths, each deeper than the last
- Say SHAH - TAHM - RAH slowly and with intent
- Trace this symbol on each of your palms and chakras
- See the symbol in your mind over and over again
- Keep saying the word SHAH - TAHM - RAH with the intention to invoke powerful Lemurian healing for protection
- Continue this for five to ten minutes or as long as you feel necessary
- Keep protecting yourself when you are out and about this week and see if you can feel a difference. Once attuned, try tracing this on your client's chakras to help them protect too.

PEARLS OF WISDOM

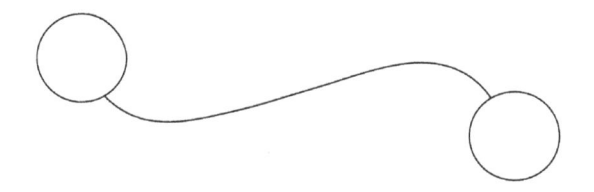

Symbol name: Pearls of wisdom

Meaning: Insight to your soul purpose

Symbol chant: OH - MAH - NAHM - RAH

This is a very an exciting symbol. This helps to connect you to the universe during a healing session. This encourages you to find your soul's purpose or next step. You may be drawn to this course as you want to find your way in life, this symbol may help with this. This symbol is powerful, however your purpose may be revealed to you slowly. I would not suggest using this symbol more than once a week. As the universe may take a few days to fully communicate with your soul. So it may be a while before you start to understand your true soul's purpose on this Earth.

Lemurian healing is about becoming one with all things and beings. It is predominantly about unity. This symbol helps us connect to other souls and to the universe itself. If you are going to become a certified Lemurian healing teacher you may then use this healing symbol on clients. Please ensure you state to your clients that you are going to be using this healing symbol in your sessions and that it is powerful. Please also ensure you get the clients permission to use this symbol on them.

Process:
- Ensure you are sitting or lying comfortably
- Ask Amara in your mind to be with you during the healing session
- I would suggest using this symbol to find your soul purpose
- Take three deep breaths, each deeper than the last
- Say OH - MAH - NAHM - RAH slowly and with intent
- Trace this symbol on each of your palms and chakras
- See the symbol in your mind over and over again
- Keep saying the word OH - MAH - NAHM - RAH with the intention to invoke powerful Lemurian healing to help find your soul purpose
- Continue this for five to ten minutes or as long as you feel necessary

- Meditate this week, have some quiet time and see if your soul purpose information starts to come through. This may take time, so keep trying. When attuned you can also trace this on your client's chakras with their permission.

Tiff's Top Tips on Using The Symbols

- You may want to have the symbols written down near you to enhance your connection.
- Some people put the symbols above their door or on their healing couch to help with healing, especially the Amara symbol.
- Please ensure you are in a meditative state before you start to use the symbols.
- Please ensure you have fully opened your chakras before using the symbols, you may have your own technique for this.

- Please drink plenty of water before and after each ceremony for cleansing.
- If you have healing crystals such as quartz or amethyst, you may want to have these near you now.
- The Lemurian seed crystal will be an excellent crystal to have on your persons during the healing session but it is not compulsory.
- Ensure you take three deep breaths before you begin, each deeper than the last.
- You may want to remind yourself of the Lemurian age before you start to use the symbols.
- Don't worry if you don't 'feel' Amara around you. Just trust she is there.
- Always state the intention that you are going to invoke healing from Lemuria before you start. Trust it is working.
- Please take your time whilst fully opening your chakras properly.

- Only once you have done this are you ready to start using the symbols.
- You may want to use the symbols daily at first (except for the pearls of wisdom which can't be used more than once a week).
- Ensure you are fully aware of each symbol and what each symbol represents.
- Only once you are an accredited teacher, can you do the same on a client.
- You don't have to work with all the symbols. You may find you just use the power symbol 'Amara' to open up, then use the symbol you need.

Closing Down Exercise

Closing down must be done at the end of each ceremony. Here's one way to close down.

It is very important to close down after each Lemurian healing session. This is so that your chakras are not left wide open. If left open, you may feel uneasy and disorientated. It can also leave you wide open for others to 'get inside' your energy field which can lead to you feeling drained. Being wide open all of the time can also be distracting.

Are you ready to try closing down now?

Sit up straight and relax.

Feel your whole body relax from your toes to your forehead – take your time with this, breathe deeply.

Now To Close Down:

- Imagine putting up a shield of white energy followed by gold energy around your whole body, leaving you in a bubble of white and gold light like a cocoon.

- Thank yourself, your higher self, any guides you may or may not have called upon or encountered and thank the universe for being present during the chakra opening session.

- Start with your base chakra at the base of your spine. Imagine a black cloth being put over the swirling red circle and feel this chakra get smaller while holding the intent to close your base chakra.

- Focus your energy on your orange sacral chakra below your navel, ask your higher self to close this down, feeling the orange circle getting smaller and the circular swirl getting slower.

- Imagine a shield over your solar plexus chakra above your navel. See the yellow swirl start to fade. Get a padlock and lock the shield holding the intent to fully close your solar plexus chakra. Do not move on until you feel the yellow circle stop swirling around.

- Focus your energy on the pink and green swirling energy around your heart centre. Ask your higher self to close your heart chakra now, with love. Feel the energy contracting.

- Stop the blue swirl at your throat chakra and watch it disappear.

- Focus all your energy on closing down your third eye in the middle of your forehead. Imagine the Indigo coloured swirl stopping as your brow chakra closes down.

- Imagine a lotus flower above the top of your head. Imagine the petals of this flower closing as you close down your crown chakra.

- Place a clear silk sheet over your entire body in your mind.

- Imagine a green shower of light washing over you as you close down entirely.

- See your energy coming out of the ethers and coming back into your body.

- Cut all ties if you have a client with you and separate from the client's aura.

- Declare that the session is over and your senses are now shut down. You can say this in your mind if you wish.

- Imagine bricks on the bottom of your feet for the rest of the day to ground you.

Exercise

Try opening and closing at least five times this week before moving on to the next stage.

Unblock Emotions

Please wait at least seven days before moving on to this section of the course.

This course will not only help you to re balance your chakras but also to heal clients, both physically and emotionally. This healing course can help to heal anything. Lemurian healing can aid both physical and emotional issues. We are now going to look at emotional healing. Not only will it help you and your clients to find blocked emotions but it can also help you heal emotional blockages that you may not even be aware of. Join me now in a deep meditation to assist you in emotional blocks.

Exercise

I would like you to lay down and take three deep breaths in, each deeper than the last. I want you to concentrate very carefully as we are about to go on a journey. Please state the intention that you are about to set free any blockages you have from past or present incidences in your life.

As you keep your eyes closed I want you to imagine that your soul has stepped out of your body. Imagine you are purely a soul right now. See the room you are in. See your body in front of you and see the clothes you are wearing. Hear any noise from outside the house. Look down and notice the floor. As you look to your left, you notice that there is a being there that wasn't there before. This is Archangel Gabriel. Imagine this now. You can see this beautiful, loving angel in your mind's eye. Notice what he looks like. See what comes to you as you feel or see him. Notice how you feel being in his presence. You can see a huge white ray of light surrounding him now. This ray is pure source energy. This ray of light is bringing you joy, grace, clarity, understanding, generosity and it's bringing you order in to your life.

Archangel Gabriel lengthens his hand to you now. He wants to take you on a journey. As you take his hand you immediately start to rise upwards. You leave your room, your house, the Earth floor. You can now see the Earth getting smaller and smaller. Gabriel is taking you to his Archangel retreat for purification. You enjoy flying with Gabriel for a few moments. You then feel Archangel Gabriel slowing down. You are nearly at your destination. You are travelling through a white vortex of light. Gabriel makes a slowing motion and starts to walk forwards so you join him.

Gabriel walks through what seems to be a white tunnel of purity. You can see the end of the tunnel and you know that you are heading there. As you leave the tunnel you are surrounded by huge trees called Redwoods. You can see them all around you and strangely you can see many of them beneath you as if you are way up in the sky.

Archangel Gabriel explains that you are at his retreat above Mount Shasta. You are able to come back here at any time for purification. As you stay very still, take three deep breaths. Feel Lemurian healing energy running through you now. Feel the energy going to parts of your body that have previously felt both physical and emotional pain. This may be in your heart, your head, your back, your shoulders, or this could be all over you. Hold the intention to purify all these areas of your body. These areas may again hurt slightly as the pain leaves your body. Feel your aura clear now. If there are certain blockages that you still struggle with, ask Angel Gabriel now to help clear these for you. Hold the intention with confidence that these ailments will not return. Know the power of intention can help with any ailment or blockage right now.

Bask in Archangel Gabriel's energy for five to ten minutes. Ask if he has a message for you. This could be a message of love, kindness, healing or anything else. Feel this now.

Know that it is time to leave Mount Shasta. Thank Gabriel for this wonderful experience. Know that he will welcome you back for purification at any time. Thank Gabriel now and offer love to the motherland and to the

Archangels. You start to fly back through the white vortex. You see the Earth getting larger. You then see the original room you started from. You become aware that you are about to come back down to Earth.

Hold the intention to start to come back in to the room now. You will do this slowly at your own pace. Start by wiggling your fingers and toes. Start to remember your surroundings in the room you are in. Start to remember what you are going to do with the rest of your day, who you have to talk to or see. Take three short sharp breaths and open your eyes. Wrap yourself in a beautiful bubble of white light and ground yourself for the rest of the day by pretending there are heavy weights on your feet.
Ensure you fully close down once this exercise is complete.

Exercise

Note your emotions this week. Are you feeling vulnerable, sad, anxious, low? Open all the chakras one by one and ask yourself why you are feeling this way. Ask yourself how to heal yourself. Note your findings. Perhaps you just feel happiness or excitement? Note the reasons why when opening your chakras.

Final meditation with Amara

Please ensure you recap on all sections of this course and wait seven days at least before moving on to this section.

Thank you for joining me on this wonderful journey to learn the powerful healing techniques of Lemuria. I would like end this course with a meditation.

Meditation

Start to breathe slowly releasing your day's events. Let go of your daily chores and worries. See everything you need to do today in front of you and put it all in a treasure chest. You know that you need to complete these things but, for now, we are going to lock the chest. Take three deep breaths as you remove negativity from your body. Just concentrate on the sound of your breath.

See yourself standing in front of Amara. See her smiling down on you now. Feel her presence. What does she look like? Examine her face as much as you are able to. She will look different to everyone.

Amara is pointing at something in the distance. You look ahead. She is pointing at a huge mountain. This is Mount Shasta. She offers her hand out to you to take you there. You feel her kindness and warmth and you feel safe going with her.

As you walk with Amara you notice how blue the sky is. Look at all of the huge trees around you now. The leaves on the trees are just turning orange and red for autumn time. Examine the leaves on the floor as you walk toward the mountain with Amara. As you look to the mountain, you can see a purple haze all around this sacred place. You notice something around the mountain that looks like a big purple triangle. Take note of the purple triangle over the mountain now. Feel the healing coming from this area.

Amara is quiet and thoughtful. You get a sense from her that this is your spiritual journey. Amara is silently helping you on your spiritual path, holding the space for you to grow.

As you climb higher up the mountain it becomes colder; stay close to Amara to keep warm. You can hear something in the distance. It sounds like a choir of angels singing as you get closer to the top of the mountain. The singing is beautiful and inviting. You feel like there are angels and guides waiting for you, you feel like the singing is a greeting, a calling.

As you look to the top of the path you are climbing, you can see a friendly face looking at you. This is Adama. He is wearing his usual white robes. His long blonde hair sits by his shoulders and his blue eyes are hard to miss. He stands holding his hands out to you.

As you get closer to Adama feel his great presence. Feel the healing energy oozing from him. Take note of how you feel now. Take three deep breaths and fill your whole being with Adama's energy. Thank Adama for inviting you to the Lemurian mountain. Adama requests you heal for the highest good. Adama wishes you to use your healing ability wisely. In return Adama will help you with one question.

Think of your question now. Is your question to do with your healing ability? Health? Love? Career? Think carefully as you are only allowed one question.

Say the question in your mind now and 'feel' the answer from Adama. You may have to meditate on this for a few moments; you may need to come back to the mountain a few times before you get an answer. We are all different.

Thank Adama for his help and his healing. Embrace Adama now. As you embrace, give gratitude to Adama, Amara and all the Lemurians for their healing. Give thanks to the motherland. Bask in Adama's presence for a few moments before it is time to go.

Take a deep breath as you start to walk back down the mountain. See Amara next to you smiling as you reach the bottom of the mountain trail. Now embrace Amara and thank her for her help. You turn and walk away from the mountain alone. You then state the intention that you are going to now be fully aware and alert as you start to come back in to the room. This is a powerful meditation so take your time.

As you slowly open your eyes remember the message that Adama gave to you.

Tiff's Top Tips

Sometimes I feel a pulsing in my third eye in the middle of my forehead, you may feel this too from time to time. To stop this, I imagine putting a shutter over my third eye and I pretend to put bricks on the bottom of my feet to reground and close down, try this now.

You may want to try many different closing down exercises before you are fully comfortable with one. Here is an alternative closing down exercise for you. Try this now:

Exercise
- See a violet lotus flower at the top of your head
- Watch the flower open
- This is universal energy opening and connecting to your being
- Feel your body full of universal energy
- How do you feel now that you are full of universal energy?
- Feel the energy fill your soul
- Close the lotus flower knowing you are full of prana (life force energy)
- Close down the crown chakra by putting a black silk cloth over the lotus flower
- Pretend you have roots on the bottom of your feet for the rest of the day

- Practice this five times this week
- This is a very important process and closing must be done after each Lemurian healing session in your own way, for both you and your client. Leaving your chakras open can leave you feeling ungrounded and unfocused.

Quiz

Just for fun

- What does the Amara master symbol look like?
- What symbol is good for confidence?
- Who is said to be the main remaining priest of Lemuria?
- What symbol would you use for protection?
- How old can a Lemurian live for?
- Where do the remaining Lemurians now reside?

Notes

Please use the following pages to write your own personal notes

Notes

Continuing your journey

So you've got this far, but this is just the start of your journey. Wondering what to do with your gift? Wondering where to go now?

When you feel ready to go further and only when you feel it is time I would like you to join me on our spiritual quest together at my School of Accredited Teachers.

Tiffany Wardle's Certified School Seminar offers:

- Full attunement to become a Lemurian Healing Teacher

• A chance to have all of your questions answered about your psychic development.

• The school will help you on your journey to a deeper level of Lemurian healing & psychic development.

• Your senses will be heightened as we raise the frequency of the attunement.

• During the attunement you will experience new spiritual heights to help you get to a deeper level of spirituality.

This and many other seminars are held globally. We also offer the "Psychic Like Me Certified Course."

Other Books by Tiffany Wardle

The Chakra Chapter:
Chakra Colour Therapy With The Angels
By Tiffany Wardle
Available at www.tiffanywardle.com

Psychic Like Me:
By Tiffany Wardle
Available at www.tiffanywardle.com

Lemuria The Buried Truth
By Tiffany Wardle
Available on Amazon

All published by Vintage Wisdom Ltd

Lightning Source UK Ltd.
Milton Keynes UK
UKHW031014101120
373143UK00015B/1198